21st
Century
Skills Library

CITIZENS AND THEIR GOVERNMENTS

COUNTING OUR PEOPLE

TAMRA B. ORR

United States
Census
2010

Published in the United States of America by
Cherry Lake Publishing, Ann Arbor, Michigan
www.cherrylakepublishing.com

Content Adviser
Kenneth W. Wachter, PhD, Professor of Demography and Statistics, University of
California, Berkeley

Credits
Photos: Cover and page 1, ©Jim West/Alamy; page 4, ©iStockphoto.com/bonniej;
page 6, ©iStockphoto.com/webking; page 9, ©iStockphoto.com/picture; page 10,
©iStockphoto.com/cutiebootiele; page 13, ©iStockphoto.com/HultonArchive;
page 15, ©Stock Connection Blue/Alamy; page 16, ©iStockphoto.com/GgWink;
page 17, ©MARKA/Alamy; page 18, ©ClassicStock/Alamy; page 20, ©iStockphoto.com/
AlexKosev; page 22, ©Wayne Geisler, used under license from Shutterstock, Inc.;
page 24, ©Photofusion Picture Library/Alamy; page 27, ©Jeff Greenberg/Alamy;
page 28, ©Richard Levine/Alamy; page 29, ©iStockphoto.com/Maica

Library of Congress Cataloging-in-Publication Data
Orr, Tamra.
   Counting our people / Tamra B. Orr.
      p. cm.—(Citizens and their governments)
   Includes index.
   ISBN-13: 978-1-60279-632-4
   ISBN-10: 1-60279-632-7
   1. United States—Census. 2. United States—Census—Methodology.
3. United States—Population. 4. United States—Population.
5. United States—Census, 2010. I. Title. II. Series.
   HA181.O77 2010
   317.3—dc22   2009025028

Cherry Lake Publishing would like to acknowledge
the work of The Partnership for 21st Century Skills.
Please visit *www.21stcenturyskills.org* for more information.

Printed in the United States of America
Corporate Graphics Inc.
January 2010
CLSP06

CITIZENS AND THEIR GOVERNMENTS

TABLE OF CONTENTS

CHAPTER ONE
A CONSTITUTIONAL AGREEMENT

Your school's principal has come to you with an important new assignment. He wants you to count every student in your school. You need to find out exactly how many students

How would you count all the students at your school?

are in each grade. You must record their first, middle, and last names. You will also need the age, birth date, and current address of each student. You are not allowed to use a laptop for recording any of this information. Instead, you have to handwrite everything in pen on notebook paper. The principal emphasizes that you must spell everything correctly. Be sure you don't miss a single student. Don't count the same student twice!

How would you get started? What steps would you take to make sure you did a good job?

You might gather all of the students together in the school's auditorium. That would make the job a little easier. What if your principal would not let you do that? What if you had to count all of the students as they went from room to room? Instead of being in one place, they would be scattered throughout the building. You would have to track down the ones who were at recess. And remember those in the bathrooms or eating lunch. What about the students who were absent that day? You need to get their information, too. If you counted a student sitting in the cafeteria, you would have to make sure not to count her again when she went to math class. That would throw your entire count off. You do not want to have start over!

Is your head spinning? What may have sounded like a simple job at first is really complicated. This is just a fraction of the challenge that faced a group of men in the late

18th century. They were hired to count all of the people in the United States! This count is known as a **census**.

The United States had a Constitution in place at the end of the 18th century. A constitution describes the organization and laws of a country or state. Some of the greatest minds in history worked on the U.S. Constitution. They outlined a lot of new rules and laws about how the country was to be run. One of these rules required the government to find out exactly

The U.S. Constitution is the country's most important document.

how many citizens lived in the country. It also required that the government repeat the process every 10 years. The information gathered would determine how many representatives each state should have in the House of Representatives. The House of Representatives is one of the two parts of Congress. Congress is the branch of the government that makes laws for the nation. The information would also be used to determine what taxes could be collected.

LEARNING & INNOVATION SKILLS

The requirement for a census was added to the Constitution for two main reasons. The first goal was to determine how many leaders each state could send to the House of Representatives. The second goal was to determine the amount of taxes that should be **levied** on, or collected from, the people of each state.

Today, a state's population also determines how much government money it receives. This money is used for programs such as repairing roads and supporting education. Think about it. Why is it so important that a state's census information be accurate? What's at stake for the states?

The Census Act of 1790 was signed into law by President George Washington. Seventeen U.S. Marshals were hired to do the counting. Copies of this new law were sent to each of them.

Can you imagine how difficult the job must have sounded to these men? They were U.S. Marshals. But now they were also **enumerators**, as census takers were called. Their job was one that would lead them all over a growing country. They would search high and low for families. Their job would require patience and determination. The pay was low and the rewards were few. Even so, these men headed out on horseback to go door-to-door. They asked questions and recorded the answers. The first census of the United States was underway.

21ST CENTURY CONTENT

It took a long time for the first enumerators to visit every home in the country. Now, census forms are mailed out to each household. This has made the census a much faster and simpler process. Can you think of other ways the census could be improved in the future? Do you think census forms could eventually be sent out over the Internet? Why or why not?

President George Washington helped to create the earliest census in the United States.

CHAPTER TWO
TAKING NAMES AND MAKING MISTAKES

The year 1790 brought many firsts for the country. The first U.S. **patent** was granted to an inventor named Samuel Hopkins. The first successful cotton mill began operation in

Cotton mills were getting their start when the first census was created.

Rhode Island. President George Washington delivered the nation's first State of the Union speech.

That year, a nationwide census was added to the list of firsts. The enumerators rode their horses throughout the original 13 states: Connecticut, Delaware, Georgia, Maryland, Massachusetts, New Hampshire, New Jersey, New York, North Carolina, Pennsylvania, Rhode Island, South Carolina, and Virginia. They went to the districts of Maine, Vermont, and Kentucky. They also visited the territory that is now Tennessee. Traveling was not easy. Sometimes it was even dangerous. Marshals often had to ride into areas where they could get lost. They sometimes met with people who did not necessarily want to be found, let alone counted!

These determined workers were assigned the job of asking six questions:

- What is the name of the head of the household?
- How many free white males age 16 and older live here?
- How many free white males under age 16 live here?
- How many free white females live here?
- How many other free persons live here?
- How many slaves live here?

For each answer, they wrote the information down on whatever paper they were able to find. Did they write the information down correctly? No one can say for sure. We know that the risk of error was huge. It was easy to make a spelling mistake. Many of the people being questioned were

illiterate and unable to point out an error. Some were new to the United States and could not speak the language well. Some people lied about their ages. Because proof was never required, the lies slid by unnoticed. Still others did not trust the marshals—or the government. They refused to answer any questions at all, even at risk of a fine. What if a family member happened to be away? Other family members were expected to provide information about the missing person. How accurate the answers were is unclear.

The census reports were finally signed and turned in. The numbers were added up. Each African American slave was counted as only three-fifths of a person. This continued until the Fourteenth Amendment to the Constitution was approved in 1868. Native Americans, who were excluded from paying taxes, were not counted at all. The first official census revealed that the country had 3.9 million people.

Both President Washington and his secretary of state, Thomas Jefferson, were surprised at the final number. They suspected that it was too low. It was, however, the nation's first attempt at counting its citizens.

A new census was conducted every 10 years as required. The process changed and improved each time. The government learned what did and did not work from earlier censuses. By 1830, printed questionnaires were being used. A few years later, directions on how to ask the questions were created and taught to the enumerators.

African Americans were not fully counted in the first census. They did not have the right to vote, either.

The forms were huge. They measured 12 by 18 inches (30.5 by 45.7 centimeters). Along with the forms, enumerators carried pens, portable inkstands, and bottles of ink. As the process changed, so did the kind and number of questions being asked. The first census had 6 questions. The list had grown to more than 70 questions by 1840. Questions about agriculture, mining, and fishing were added. The government wanted to learn more about its people. It wanted to know how they lived.

In 1880, Congress created an official census office in Washington, DC. Professional census recorders replaced the U.S. marshals.

LIFE & CAREER SKILLS

Early in the census's history, census takers had to swear an oath. They promised to protect the privacy of all of the information they were given. They still take that oath today. They cannot reveal to anyone anything they learn. If they break this promise, they could go to prison for as long as 5 years. Or they might have to pay a fine of up to $250,000.

Can you think of some traits that good census takers should have? Being responsible, honest, and **ethical** are just a few. After all, protecting personal information is very important.

Ten years later, the process changed even more. Simple machines were used to **tabulate** all the numbers.

United States
Census
2000

This is the off
easy, and you
help your com.

Start Here

1. How many people were living or staying in th
house, apartment, or mobile home on A

Please us
black or b

Number of people

INCLUDE in this
• foster child
• people
no oth
• peo

DO NO

*Modern census forms are much
simpler than earlier versions.*

One of the first types used was the Hollerith machine. With this system, hole-punched cards were fed into the machine and counted. Hollerith machines were an important early step toward the development of digital computers. Although the Hollerith machine helped to speed up the process, even bigger changes were still ahead.

Hollerith machines used punch cards much like these.

Hollerith machines were much larger than modern-day computers.

CHAPTER THREE
LEARNING FROM THE NUMBERS

Through the years, technology became a more and more important part of the census process. During World War II

A UNIVAC computer could take up an entire room.

(1939–1945), interest in digital computers had begun to grow. From 1943 to 1946, the National Defense Research Council focused on building a computer. It was called ENIAC (for Electronic Numerical Integrator and Computer). Soon the technology developed into a line of electronic digital computers called UNIVAC (for Universal Automatic Computer). By 1960, computers were an important part of the census process.

Today, anyone can go online to find information about locating census records. It can be found at the U.S. National Archives and Records Administration Web site. Personal information about people is not included. That is not made available to the public until 72 years after the census. In other words, the details from the 2000 census will be fully released in 2072.

Every 10 years, the U.S. Census Bureau conducts its huge national head count. What does it do in between those years? It counts subgroups of the population. For example, every month of every year since 1942, it has conducted the Current Population Survey. It provides **data** on employment. It also helps determine what income level qualifies as poverty in this country. On years ending in '2' or '7,' the Economic Census is sent out. This examines U.S. businesses and looks at what the country's **economy** is doing. In addition, the Census of Governments collects information on government employment, organization, and other factors.

There are millions of details found in the more than 200 years of census records. These details have helped many historians, journalists, and government agencies find the information they need. The rows of numbers paint a picture of the country's people as the nation grew. Not only do they reflect the changes in population, but they also provide a wealth of other information. This includes how many people moved into and out of the country. It also includes how incomes

Census records are an important research tool for many people.

rose and fell over the years and what jobs people held. Most important, the census numbers have helped the country's government better understand its people. The data helps determine how the individual states should be represented and financially supported.

LEARNING & INNOVATION SKILLS

In August 1992, Hurricane Andrew hit southern Florida. How did relief workers estimate how many people might be missing in each block? How did they know how the neighborhoods were laid out and where houses had once been? Difficult situations call for creative thinking. So workers got much of their information and maps from a source that many people would not expect: census data. Census data helped highlight the number of people who lived in the hardest hit areas. It also helped determine how resources should be set aside for emergency planning and recovery efforts.

CHAPTER FOUR
CENSUS 2010

"Counting Everyone Once—and Only Once—and in the Right Place" is the motto for the 2010 census. What is the goal of a census? Getting people to respond!

U.S. census forms are mailed out every 10 years.

Despite many challenges throughout the years, the U.S. Census has been very successful. In recent decades it has counted more than 98 percent of the population. The Census Bureau works very hard to count everyone. That includes groups that may be hard to track down, such as the homeless.

For decades, the U.S. Census added more and more questions to its forms. At one point, it reached several hundred questions. It took years for experts to analyze all of the information. The Census Bureau used to have two kinds of census forms: a long-form questionnaire and a short-form questionnaire. In 2000, 5 out of every 6 households in the United States received a short form. It asked only 7 basic questions. The other households received the long form. It asked questions about 34 different topics. Questions about income, migration, work status, home value, and plumbing facilities were included.

For the 2010 census, the decision was made to send out only a short-form questionnaire. It asks about name, gender, age, and race. It also asks about **ethnicity**, relationship to the head of household, and if the home is rented or owned. The form can be filled out in about 10 minutes. The government's goal for using the short form is to get more people to complete it by the deadline.

Census forms are mailed to every household throughout the United States, the District of Columbia, Puerto Rico, and the Island Areas. Thirteen million of the forms are printed in

Spanish and English. The Census Bureau also makes forms available in Chinese, Korean, Vietnamese, and Russian. These forms help those who struggle with reading and writing English. No one is asked to prove his or her legal status. This way, every **immigrant** can be counted on the census.

So what does this mean for you? After your family receives the short printed form in the mail, it will have to

The census form only takes a few minutes to fill out, but it is a very helpful tool.

be filled out. A member of your family, often your father or mother, will enter his or her name as the head of household. Some of the lines ask specifically for information about you. You will be asked to indicate your gender, age, and your relationship to the person listed as the head of household. There are other lines that ask about your race and ethnicity. Your answers about race and ethnicity are up to you. This kind of reporting is called self-identification. Many people may have to think about how to answer that section. Do you, for example, have parents or grandparents of different races or ethnic backgrounds?

Since 2000, the U.S. Census form has allowed you to mark more than one choice to indicate race. This makes it easier for many people to choose the response that best represents them.

People are given about 1 month to fill out the forms and return them. Anyone who does not turn in the form will be sent a second one. If that is not filled in and mailed, an enumerator will either call or visit the home to get the answers.

Does the small number of questions on the new census form mean that the government is no longer interested in all of that extra information? Not at all. Much of that information is gathered through the other types of questionnaires that are sent out. After years of testing, the Census Bureau fully launched the American Community Survey between 2005 and 2006. This survey is sent out every month to a sample of the population. Three million U.S. households receive the survey each year. It has questions about people's professions, incomes, and other topics.

21ST CENTURY CONTENT

Keeping accurate population records is important to governments around the world. In Canada, for example, the first census was taken in 1666. The first national census did not begin until 1871. The census was established through the country's Constitution. It is held every 10 years. Beginning in 1956, Canada has had mini-censuses, held every 5 years. Today, Canada's census is held within each one of its 10 provinces and 3 territories.

Which countries do you think have the largest populations? Which have the smallest? Where can you find this census information?

Counting the nation's people is much more complicated than counting all of the students in your school. But it is worth the trouble. It was considered important enough two centuries ago that it was described in the U.S. Constitution.

The U.S. Census Bureau is always looking for better ways to count the nation's people.

Today, it is as important as ever. How do you think the ways census information is collected and processed will change in the years to come? How might new forms of technology make gathering data faster, easier, and more accurate? Think ahead to the future. In what ways might the 2100 census show us how the country and its people have changed? Only time will tell!

The U.S. Census Bureau works hard to make sure citizens understand the importance of the census.

Now that you know how a census is done, what new ideas do you have for counting the students at your school?

GLOSSARY

census (SEN-suhss) an official count of all of the people living in a country

data (DAY-tuh) information or facts

economy (i-KON-uh-mee) the way a country runs its industry, trade, and finance

enumerators (i-NOO-muh-ray-turz) census takers, or people who collect census data by visiting individual homes

ethical (ETH-uh-kuhl) having to do with following moral rules of behavior

ethnicity (eth-NIH-sih-tee) the background, culture, and language shared by a group of people

illiterate (i-LIT-ur-it) not able to read or write

immigrant (IM-uh-gruhnt) someone who comes from one country to live permanently in another country

levied (LEV-eed) collected by force or lawful actions

patent (PAT-uhnt) a legal document that gives an inventor of something new the exclusive rights to make and sell the item

tabulate (TAB-yuh-late) to arrange or enter information in columns and rows

FOR MORE INFORMATION

BOOKS

Anderson, Judith. *Ways to Do Surveys*. North Mankato, MN: Smart Apple Media, 2008.

Taylor-Butler, Christine. *The Constitution*. New York: Children's Press, 2008.

Thomas, Isabel. *Graphing Population*. Chicago: Heinemann Library, 2009.

WEB SITES

U.S. Census Bureau—About 2010 Census
2010.census.gov/2010census/about_2010_census/
Discover links and information on the 2010 census.

U.S. Census Bureau—Census in Schools: Census for Kids
www.census.gov/schools/census_for_kids/
Find fun activities and a quiz on census topics.

U.S. Census Bureau—FactFinder Kids' Corner
factfinder.census.gov/home/en/kids/kids.html
Find more information on why the census is important along with state population facts.

INDEX

ABOUT THE AUTHOR

Tamra B. Orr is a full-time writer living in the Pacific Northwest. She is the author of more than 200 nonfiction books for readers of all ages. Several of her titles have won awards. She lives with her children, husband, cat, and dog and is sure that every day, when she takes her own census, the number keeps growing.